台灣蘭花
Orchids in Taiwan

克利斯多福 歐肯姆瓦詩集
Collection of Poems by Christopher Okemwa

李魁賢漢譯
Translated into Mandarin by Lee Kuei-shien

First Edition: September 2024
Published by: Nsemia Inc. Publishers (www.nsemia.com)

Translated by: Lee Kuei-shien
Cover Concept & Illustration:
Cover Design: Linda Kiboma
Layout Design: Bethsheba Nyabuto

Note for Librarians:
A cataloguing record for this book is available from Kenya National Library Services

ISBN: 978-9914-760-16-3

詩讓我們永遠在一起！

Poetry will keep us together forever!

Table of Contents

ENGLISH TRANSLATION

《台灣蘭花》前言 李魁賢

　　閱讀肯亞詩人克利斯多福．歐肯姆瓦詩集《台灣蘭花》，被他對台灣的深情感動不已，對他詩中運用的逆說表達技巧，以旁敲側擊的手段，引導讀者墜入他設計的圈套中，更是不斷驚嘆，這種以反諷的陳述方式，加強正面肯定的態度，產生令人意料不到的驚奇效果。

　　例如首篇的〈我不想去台灣〉，題目即表明反面立場，詩起頭就明指台灣如墳場，是殺人如麻的地方，內容歷述獨裁者蔣介石、毛澤東的惡行，相對地對台灣先賢林獻堂與辜振甫的精神給予肯定，怕打擾他們永恆安息，接著說不想挑起，實際上反而是在張揚黃紀男爭取獨立和自由的台灣歷史，循線細數史明上街頭的激進運動和抗議，彭明敏發表〈臺灣自救運動宣言〉遭到逮捕、入獄，然後流亡國外，又涉及到雷震主張「中華台灣民主國」，這些都是事關台灣獨立運動，詩人受到感動流淚，因為他還不致於麻木不仁。

　　實際上，可見詩人所謂不想去台灣，是因為他惋惜台灣還不能名正言順獨立，他受不了台灣的黑暗記憶。這種抒情詩帶有史詩的意圖，非常獨特，或許可稱為史詩式抒情詩，在〈台灣〉這首詩裡翻閱台灣像圖畫書，「走過大肚王國／清朝／走過東寧王國／國姓爺府／到福爾摩莎共和國」，敘述以蜻蜓點水式跳越過去，在史詩發展上還留有空白，等待填補。

　　克利斯多福．歐肯姆瓦於2023年應邀來台灣參加淡水福爾摩莎國際詩歌節，趁便深入理解台灣歷史和政治現況，例如詩寫烈士〈湯德章〉殉難，「坂井德章呀／雖然有日本血統／站在我們身邊／…／成為我們的人／…／為我們的獨立／受苦、蒙羞／你放棄呼吸／在台南殉道／在你最愛的國家」，又以〈自焚〉寫鄭南榕，「用你的身體和心靈／你堅定的精神／用火給自己施洗／化為灰燼／為防止被捕／為抗議中華民國」。詩人完全身以台灣人的立場，寫出台灣追求獨立的慘痛歷程，感同身受，而詩人的敏銳觀察和感受，能夠親身融入台灣社會體驗台灣人民的心聲，更是令人深深佩服。

　　詩人克利斯多福．歐肯姆瓦不但寫台灣歷史，凸顯台灣人的奮鬥努力精神，也描寫台灣民俗和豐富物產，例如〈在台灣，夢想長在樹上〉刻畫台灣人「在元宵節跳舞／敬拜往生的祖先／享受元宵湯圓」，「農曆新年時／家族共享豐盛的年夜飯」，用冥幣「供奉往生的祖先」，而「喪事期間／遊蕩的亡靈／因鋼管舞和脫衣舞表演／受到安撫，不會害人」，都讓他感到台灣人心溫暖。在〈楓葉〉詩裡記錄他參訪過汐止拱北殿，以及在台灣民間到處受人民景仰的「觀世音菩薩、關公和土地公」的廟宇，而幻想這些神祇肉身仍活在世間保佑人民。

詩人遊台灣，遍歷山水間，看盡美麗山河，在〈楓葉〉裡「走入太平山森林」、「攀登誘人的拉拉山」、「去一座小山頂／馬那邦山」，在〈夜幕降臨台北〉裡提到七星山，也仰望玉山，照顧到濁水溪，〈神住在台灣〉裡更指涉到玉山、秀姑巒溪、達芬尖山、太魯閣峽谷、立霧溪、十分瀑布、東埔溫泉村、武陵農場、七星山、十八羅漢山、梨山風景區、阿里山森林，瀏覽這些名勝風景區內的動植物，獼猴、赤腹松鼠、櫻花樹、蘋果、桃和梨，〈台灣蘭花〉更是對享譽國際的蘭花逐一點名，四重溪脈葉蘭、天麻、玉山一葉蘭、劍心蘭、長腳羊耳蒜、台灣香莢蘭、春蘭，詩人也忍不住一再讚賞「台灣呀／真是蘭花之鄉」！

克利斯多福．歐肯姆瓦對台灣的喜愛與讚賞，採用精彩的逆說表達技巧，已如開宗明義所述，比正面的讚美描寫，更加出奇制勝，翻轉力道更強大。例如〈降落台灣〉是對台灣的見面禮，飛機到達台灣要降落時，由於雜音最大，詩人想像飛機似乎遭遇亂流等重大事故，就要解體，險象環生，漸漸進逼，令讀者提心吊膽，尤其是最後緊張到全副神經緊繃，「最後一聲巨響／輪胎沿跑道尖叫／在飛機過度忍耐時／可以聽到爆發憤怒聲」，隨即急轉直下，原來已安全著陸，「台灣，我們的非洲來啦！／台灣，我們的詩來啦！」歡欣鼓舞的精神，表現無遺！

在〈我本來沒打算到台灣〉裡，逆說的表達技巧發揮到淋漓盡致，處處以美國的名勝反襯出台灣之美。詩人本來沒打算到台灣，而是計劃前往美國遊亞利桑那州大峽谷，結果來台灣發現日月潭神奇的自然美景，讓他「簡直愛上台灣啦」。詩人本來沒打算到台灣，而是計劃前往美國遊加州優勝美地國家公園，結果來台灣發現九份老街，享受民間美食，讓他「確實驚奇來到台灣啦」。詩人本來沒打算到台灣，而是計劃前往美國遊紐約摩天大樓，結果來台灣發現台北101層摩天大樓，還有龍山寺層層瀑布、錦鯉魚池，讓他「忘掉紐約市摩天大樓啦」。詩人本來沒打算到台灣，而是計劃前往美國遊猶他州錫安國家公園，結果來台灣發現太魯閣國家公園，讓他「不敢相信竟然身在台灣」。詩人最初是夢想去華盛頓特區，結果來台灣高雄發現澄清湖和壽山，讓他「全忘掉華盛頓特區啦」。詩人始終想去洛杉磯，結果來台灣發現饒河街夜市萬事俱備的地方，讓他「全忘掉洛杉磯啦」。以如此反比，強化來台灣的決定是正確的，毫不後悔，詩人對台灣人文地理的肯定，足堪擔任台灣文化大使。

詩人克利斯多福．歐肯姆瓦對台灣的愛，甚至在〈如果我繪妳〉中，把台灣繪成非洲女人，攜帶小葫蘆，在餵孩子，有強壯的背，堅挺的脖子，頭髮黑如灰燼，臉上陽光燦爛，嘴唇有笑容，臉頰有酒窩，門牙有間隙，右臂揹鏢槍，左臂擺盾牌，腰部繫非洲珠串，手腕戴手鐲，脖子掛金鍊條。哇！完全一副令人嚮往的非洲美女形象，而且文武雙全。在詩人想像中，台灣之美宜成為神仙之鄉，所以〈神住在台灣〉，在此詩中描寫台灣風景秀麗、物產豐富、人民勤奮、社會安寧，所以結尾是「神愛台灣住在台灣」。而詩人假設〈如果我必須住在台灣〉，他寧願選擇南投的自然美景，或是宜蘭山林幽趣，或是台北熱鬧都市，而這些地方也正是神在台灣的住居地方。

詩人終於還是想要離開台灣，回到非洲家裡，他為此寫兩首詩，提出兩個理由，〈我想要離開台灣（一）〉的第一個理由強調數字「四」在作祟，「四」在台灣的發音類似「死」，許多台灣人會視為禁忌，詩人克利斯多福．歐肯姆瓦受到影響，顯示他很快融入台灣社會生活，而歷述他巧遇到「四」的場合，讓他緊張，其實這是展現詩人的幽默感，也暗喻他與台灣人生活觀念的一致性。〈我想要離開台灣（二）〉的第二個理由當然是想家，想念陽光、黃昏細雨、泥路弄髒鞋子、螢火蟲、蟋蟀唧唧叫、群鳥在巢內啁啾、妻子夜晚打盹和在爐邊講故事、鄰居兒童喧鬧和尖叫聲、鬥牛比賽、村民爭吵變成打架等等，在台灣都沒有。當然，有些台灣也有，有些確實沒有，真正的問題是，人走天下，終究要回家，神可以選擇住在香格里拉，人還是不能長久離家　　。但天涯若比鄰，詩心無遠勿屆，詩讓我們永遠在一起！

2024年7月5日

Foreword to "Orchids in Taiwan" by Lee Kuei-shien

In reading the poetry book "Orchids in Taiwan" written by Kenyan poet Christopher Okenmwa, I was deeply moved by his deep affection for Taiwan, and constantly amazed by his paradoxical expression techniques utilized in his poems to guide readers into the trap designed by his measure of insinuations. This ironic statement manner strengthens the positive and affirmative attitude, and produces unexpected and surprising effects.

Take the first poem "I Don't Want to Go to Taiwan" for example, its title expresses a negative stance. At the beginning of the poem, it is clearly stated that Taiwan is like a graveyard, a place where many people are killed. The content recounts the evil deeds of dictators Chiang Kai-shek and Mao Zedong, and relatively the spirit of the Taiwanese sages Lin Hsien-tang and Koo Chen-fu is affirmed, avoiding to disturb their eternal rest. Then it mentions that the poet does not want to arouse, but in fact on the contrary to promote the history of Taiwan in struggle for independence and freedom initiated by Ńg Kí-lâm. Following the context, this poem describes Su Beng getting back to the streets for activism and protests, Peng Ming-min issued "A Declaration of Formosan Self-salvation" and was arrested, jailed, then pardoned and sent into exile abroad, and Lei Chen advocated the "The Democratic State of China-Taiwan". These were all related to the movement of Taiwan independence. The poet was moved to shed tears because he is not sufficiently callous.

In fact, it can be seen that the reason why the poet does not want to go to Taiwan is because he regrets that Taiwan cannot yet be legitimately independent, and he "can't stand the dark memories of Taiwan". This kind of lyric poem has an epic intention and is very unique, it may be called an epic style lyric poem. In the poem "Taiwan", open Taiwan like a picture book and «walks through the Kingdom of Middag/Qing Dynasty/ through the Kingdom of Tungning/House of Koxinga/to the Republic of Formosa", the narrative skips over the past, like the dragonfly touches the water lightly, leaving gaps in the development of the epic waiting to be filled.

Christopher Okemwa was invited to Taiwan in 2023 to participate in the Formosa International Poetry Festival held in Tamsui, he gained a deep understanding of Taiwan's history and current political situation, such as he took the opportunity to write a poem about the martyrdom of the martyr "Tang Te-Chang" that "Sakai Tokusho/Although with a Japanese blood/You stood by us/.../And became one of us/.../For our independence/Tortured and humiliated/You gave up your breath/You died in Tainan/In the nation you loved most" , and to write about Cheng Nan-jung in the poem of "Immolation" that «With your body and soul/your determined spirit/you baptize yourself with fire/turning into cinders/to prevent arrest/to protest against the ROC". Standing completely as a Taiwanese, the poet writes about Taiwan's painful process in pursuing independence with his empathetic. The poet's keen observations and feelings, and able to personally integrate into Taiwanese society for the experience of the voices of the Taiwanese people, are deeply admirable.

Poet Christopher Okemwa not only writes about the history of Taiwan and highlights the struggle and hardworking spirit of Taiwanese people, but also describes Taiwanese folk customs and rich products. For example, "In Taiwan, Dreams Grow on Trees" depicts Taiwanese people "dance in the lantern festival/and honour the dead ancestors/relish yuanxiao and tangyuan", "in the Lunar New Year/you share in a sumptuous meal as families", use Hell Banknote "to support the dead ancestors" and "during the funeral ceremonies,/the wandering spirits of the dead are appeased, made harmless/ by pole dancers and strippers", all let him feel warm in all hearts of Taiwanese people. In the poem "Maple Leaves", he records that he visited Xizhi Gongbei Temple and the temples of "Guanyin Bodhisattva, Guan Gong, and the Earth God" that are admired by people everywhere in Taiwan, and "see in a vision" that these gods are still alive in the world to protect the people.

The poet traveled to Taiwan, traversing among the mountains and rivers, and saw all the beautiful territory. In "Maple Leaves", he walked "into Taiping Mountain forest", climbed up "the alluring La-la mountain", and went to "a miniature peaks, too/Manabang Shan». In "Nightfall in Taipei" he mentioned Mount Shichisei, looked up to the Yushan, and looked after Zhuoshui River. In "God Lives in Taiwan" he also refers to Jade Mountain, Xiuguluan River, Dafenjian Mountain, Taroko Gorge, Liwu River, Shifen Waterfall, Dongpu Hot Springs Village, Wuling Farm, Mount Qixing, Shihba Luohan Shan, Lishan Scenic Area, Alishan Forest, to browse the flora and fauna in these scenic spots, including macaques, red-bellied squirrels, cherry trees, apples, peaches and pears. In "Orchids of Taiwan» he takes a roll call the internationally renowned orchids one by one, such as Nervilia crociformis, gastrodia elata, Hemipilia cruciate, Tolumnia, Liparis condylobulbon, Vanilla somae, and Cymbidium goeringii. The poet couldn't help but praise it again and again "What a land of orchids/ Oh Taiwan"!

Christopher Okemwa loves and admires Taiwan by using wonderful paradoxical techniques as stated clearly at the beginning. It is more surprising and more powerful than the positive description of praise. For example, the poem of "Landing in Taiwan" is a greeting to Taiwan. When the plane arrived Taiwan and was about to land, the noise was the loudest. The poet imagined that the plane seemed to have encountered a major accident such as turbulence and was about to disintegrate. The dangers were everywhere and gradually approaching, making the readers a great fear, especially at the end, when all the nerves were tense, "finally a big bang/The tires screamed along the runway/The fury of the plane could be heard/As its overstretched patience bursts out". Then the situation is overturned abruptly, and it turned out to be a safe landing, "Taiwan, here comes our Africa!/ Taiwan, here comes our poetry!" The joyful spirit is fully expressed!

In "I Didn't Plan to Come to Taiwan", the expressive of paradoxical techniques are brought to full play, and the beauty of Taiwan is reflected in the American scenic spots everywhere. The poet did not plan to come to Taiwan, but planned to go to visit the canyon in Arizona. When he came to Taiwan, he discovered the magical natural beauty of Sun Moon Lake, that made him "I have simply fallen in love with Taiwan." The poet did not plan to come to Taiwan, but planned to go to visit Yosemite National Park in California. When he came to Taiwan, he discovered Jiufen Old Street and enjoyed the folk delicacies, that made him "I am surely amazed being in Taiwan!" The poet did not plan to come to Taiwan, but planned to see the skyscrapers in New York City. When he came to Taiwan, he discovered the 101-story skyscraper in Taipei, as well as cascading waterfalls and koi fish ponds in Longshan Temple, that made him "I forget all about the NYC skyscrapers." The poet did not plan to come to Taiwan, but planned to go to visit Zion National Park in Utah. However, when he came to Taiwan and discovered Taroko National Park, that made him "I became bewildered being in Taiwan!" The poet first had a dream of going to Washington DC, but when he came to Kaohsiung, Taiwan, he discovered Cheng Ching Lake and Shoushan Mountain, that made him "I forget all about Washington DC". The poet has always dream going to Los Angeles, but when he came to Taiwan, he discovered that Raohe Street Night Market was a place with everything, that made him "I forget all about Los Angeles." With such a contrast, it reinforces that the decision to come to Taiwan was correct and that he has no regrets. The poet so affirms the human geography of Taiwan that he has sufficient ability to serve as Taiwanese ambassador of culture.

Poet Christopher Okemwa loves Taiwan even in the poem of "If I Paint You" to paint Taiwan as an African woman, carrying a small calabash to feed the children, with a strong back and a solid neck, hair black like ash, with sun-lit faces, smile on lips, dimple on cheeks, gap in front teeth, spear on right arm, shield on other arm, African beads on waists, bangle on wrists, and gold chain on neck. Wow! It is a completely attractive image of an African beauty endowed with civil and martial virtues. The poet imagines that the beauty of Taiwan should become the home of gods, that made him in the poem of "God Lives in Taiwan" describing a beautiful scenery in Taiwan, there are rich products, diligent people, and peaceful society, so that "God loves and lives in Taiwan" at the end. The poet supposes «If I Must Live in Taiwan", he will prefer rather choose the beautiful landscape in nature of Nantou, the tranquility of the mountains and forests of Yilan, or the bustling city of Taipei, and these places are where God lives in Taiwan.

The poet finally wanted to leave Taiwan and return to his home in Africa. He wrote two poems for this purpose and gave two reasons. The first reason from "I Want to Leave Taiwan (I)" emphasizes that the number "four" makes trouble. In Taiwan, the pronunciation of "four" is similar to "death", which is considered taboo by many Taiwanese people. The poet Christopher Okemwa was affected, which shows that he quickly integrated into Taiwanese social life, and writing the occasions he happened to encounter about "four" that made him nervous. In fact, this shows the poet's sense of humor and also implies his consistency with life concepts of Taiwanese people. The second reason from "I Want to Leave Taiwan (II)" is of course missing home, missing sunshine, evening soft rain, the mud on roads to smudge his shoes, as well as fireflies, crickets chirp, birds sing from their nests, and to hear his wife snoring at night and telling her stories by the fireside, as well as to hear the din and screams from children in the neighbourhood, to see bull-fighting game, village people making the brawl turning into a fight, etc. are all absent in Taiwan. Of course, Taiwan has some of them, and some surely do not. The real problem is that when people travel around the world, they have to go home eventually. Gods can choose to live in Shangri-La, while people still can't leave home for a long time. But if we feel close to each other at far terminal of the world, our poetry will reach everywhere. Poetry will keep us together forever!

July 5, 2024

我不想去台灣

我不想去台灣
我還不夠冷漠
去台灣
就像
走過流淚的墳墓
散落一把骨骼的槍
和無數髑髏的一顆子彈

這會像在挖掘
蔣介石、毛澤東的
英雄骨肉
把噁心的痛苦記憶
注入我的身體

我不想去台灣
我還不夠冷酷
去台灣
就像
在喚醒林獻堂與辜振甫的
精神
使他們不安寧
我不想打擾往生者
在永恆安息寓所的心靈
使台灣再度落淚

就像
打開黃紀男墳墓
窺視黑洞
使他感到焦慮不安
我不想挑起台灣歷史
爭取獨立和自由

說實話，我不想去台灣
我容易感動流淚
如果我去台灣
就像
重新點燃獨立的禁忌議題
讓史明回到街頭
從事激進運動和抗議
逃避警察子彈
逮捕和酷刑

就像
把史明從墳墓拉出來
圖謀暗殺蔣介石
非常危險的事件
我不想容忍這些回憶
讓史明影子在我面前出現

確實，我討厭去台灣
我不想演繹台灣史
就像
讓彭明敏重生
形成他孚眾望的的裝備
〈臺灣自救運動宣言〉

把他逮捕，入獄
隨後加以赦免
把他放逐
我受不了台灣的黑暗記憶

就像
把台灣帶回到
「中華台灣民主國」
還有雷震
站在歷史講台上
演講獨立計劃
我不想去台灣
我還不夠麻木不仁
我很敏感會流淚

降落台灣

飛機似乎正在反咬
本身在顫抖、跟著打嗝
傳來怒吼，哀號雜音
假使墜毀呢—天呀！
假使機身解體
四散掉落呢？或者，有一機翼無力
或襟翼故障，或前緣縫翼裂開
或者有一擾流板散落？
天呀！—我們都會見到鬼
我聽到顫抖聲，機身在晃動
好像全部東西正在破裂
聽到翼片發出巨大聲響
襟翼、副翼、駕駛艙
正撕開雲層內部
毛皮、棉花和劍麻纖維飛逝
我們漂浮在空無黑暗中
引擎在哀號抗爭
哎喲！—東西突然掉落下來
坐在我旁邊的一位老婦
雙腿迅速壓緊座位
試圖把飛機穩定
天呀！—聽到怪異的呼嘯聲
顫抖和咯吱咯吱聲
有誰知道我們在這裡上空？
台北永遠不會知道我們的名字
他們會聽不到我們讀詩
我們將消失在宇宙中

天呀！—假使尾翼脫落？
駕駛員無法控制飛機
天呀！—我害怕—天呀！
我們將搖擺、偏離方向、迷失
也許會掉進海裡淹沒
或栽進森林被動物吞食
哎喲！—又是突然下降！
我的心跳停了一拍—天呀！
我的腸子在胃裡翻騰
我緊繫安全帶
我祈禱—或是我想哭？
機身晃動，我也跟著顫抖
引擎聲音越來越大
假使我們掉進百慕達三角洲呢？
天呀！天呀！天呀！—我害怕呀！
我們將會滅亡，消失無影無蹤
不留殘骸，無人倖存
駕駛員，我們好心的駕駛員呀，求求你
檢查那著名的無磁差線
我聽說對於磁羅盤的變化
你不該賠償—駕駛員，對吧？
天呀！—害怕心理壓垮我的整個生命
我們可能會被洶湧海浪吞噬
天呀！—突然一陣顫抖，飛機緩慢轉彎
搖晃、震動，血液在我血管裡凝固啦
機身似乎要撕裂
哎喲！—東西又突然掉下來啦
我正襟危坐在座位上，閉眼祈禱
老婦把手指緊壓住座位
極度恐怖閉著眼睛

她在哭泣—或者可能在祈禱
雲層如今已經晴朗—大大放心啦
太陽光線透射進來
又是一陣顫抖，最後一聲巨響
輪胎沿跑道尖叫
在飛機過度忍耐時
可以聽到爆發憤怒聲
台灣，我們的非洲來啦！
台灣，我們的詩來啦！

台灣人的語言

你們的語言
像瑪瑙貝殼掉到
樹枝編製的托盤上
咚咚鏘鏘
一陣亂彈音樂節拍
頓促間斷的言語
音節轟轟敲擊耳膜
你不能錯過重音
精準
清晰
像子彈爆發
迅速射出
不斷地
對耳朵表面
更猛
可以舞蹈
像鼓般
優美
迷人又浪漫

湯德章

1947年3月11日

國民黨遠遠就

聽到你心跳

知交兄弟

坂井德章呀

雖然有日本血統

站在我們身邊

高舉我們的旗幟

吸取我們的精神

成為我們的人

德章兄弟呀

沒有講過一句

背叛、不忠的話

你放棄心靈

肉體、血統和精神

為我們的獨立

受苦、蒙羞

你放棄呼吸

在台南殉道

在你最愛的國家

德昌兄弟呀

隨天使高空飛翔吧

自焚

（紀念鄭南榕）

用你的身體和心靈
你堅定的精神
用火給自己施洗
化為灰燼
為防止被捕
為抗議中華民國

像中國皇帝
可以犧牲動物
你卻自焚
奉獻你的身體
成為祭祀的羔羊
讓我們台灣人
可以擁有自由
民主與權力
鄭南榕呀
你依然活在我們心中

在台灣，夢想長在樹上

（給我的導遊范予慈）

妳幸而出生在台灣
夢成長在眼鏡蛇、番紅花上面
生命和愛情
塗繪在玫瑰和水仙花上
而韌性，像鳳凰
或者，像耶穌死亡與復活的故事
複述在紅罌粟上
妳幸而身為台灣人
能說人民的音樂語言
在元宵節跳舞
敬拜往生的祖先
享受元宵湯圓
家庭團圓
和好、安樂、寬容
你幸而生活在台灣
老人被視同錢包
裝珠寶和黃金
在這裡，李魁賢
身為教授，有發言權
而像妳這樣的青年
抓住山間的創意繆斯
和河流的智慧
妳幸而在台灣
在這裡，妳遵守冥幣的傳統

供奉往生的祖先
在這裡，農曆新年時
家族共享豐盛的年夜飯
在這裡，喪事期間
遊蕩的亡靈
因鋼管舞和脫衣舞表演
受到安撫，不會害人
妳幸而出生在台灣
這裡有太陽的魅力和優美
溫暖人心
細雨滋潤孩童的心智

我本來沒打算到台灣

我本來沒打算去台灣
已經安排飛往亞利桑那州西北部
去看又大又深的河谷
我可以在那裡徒步旅行，
泛舟和搭直升機飛越峽谷
在峽谷南緣騎自行車。

但我改變主意，來到台灣
在這裡發現日月潭
東側形似太陽
西側形似弦月
我注意到，太陽上升時，
天空轉變成粉紅色和紫色
涵碧樓，湖畔一個小點
—啊，多麼神奇的自然美景？
我簡直愛上台灣啦。

我確實本來沒打算到台灣
因為我大為興奮
要去遊加州
去看優勝美地國家公園
享受大自然的多樣性
深谷、瀑布、草地
還有巨大紅杉—全是美景！

但是—哎喲！—我反而來到台灣
我遊台北以北的九份老街
體驗神祕氛圍—懸空的薄霧
我買到珠寶、瓶瓶罐罐
吃過魚丸、芋圓或番薯圓
紅燒肉丸、紅酒滷豬肉
麻糬、糯米糕。
我確實驚奇來到台灣啦！

我本來沒打算遊台灣
本來打算去紐約市
看那些著名的摩天大樓
（台灣確定為有這種摩天大樓嗎？）
觀賞歌舞表演，享受
頂級美食和美味的城市餐

但是，天呀！我意外來到台灣
很遺憾錯過紐約市摩天大樓
但沒多久，驚喜跟著來啦：
我看到台灣101層摩天大樓
我驚呆啦，幾乎喘不過氣來！
龍山寺，也是，滾滾而來
層層瀑布、錦鯉魚池
我忘掉紐約市摩天大樓啦

我本來無意來台灣
想盡辦法要去猶他州
遊錫安國家公園
欣賞令人驚嘆的景色：
陡峭赤壁、維琴河
試試稍微健行，去騎馬
峽谷探險和騎自行車—這一切！

不巧，風把我吹到台灣
抵達時，我不知道來這裡幹什麼！
臉上擺出小小姿態，小小輕蔑
我遊太魯閣國家公園時
哇！多麼令人震驚的風景呀！
我瞻仰永恆的長春祠
驚嘆於沿海峭立的
清水斷崖
走在很受崇拜的慈母橋上
我張口結舌，喘不過氣
我不敢相信竟然身在台灣！

我最初夢想是去華盛頓特區
參觀著名的白宮
欣賞其建造完美的道路
參觀史密森國家航空
太空博物館和潮汐盆地
在約翰甘迺迪表演藝術中心
觀賞戲劇。

但，就這樣，神讓我飛到台灣
說實話，在台灣有什麼能贏過華盛頓呢？
就此沉思之際，我來到高雄市
神呀，我的心跳漏掉一拍，下巴掉下來啦！
我驚嘆於美麗的海港景色
澄清湖，布滿小島
令人屏息的壽山
我在路上碰撞到猴子
美麗的高雄市呀！
高雄呀，什麼能配得上你！
我全忘掉華盛頓特區啦

洛杉磯始終是我的夢想
我們聽說好萊塢事情
格里菲斯天文台
愛荷華號戰艦博物館
洛杉磯郡藝術博物館
內瑟克特汽車博物館中的古董車
這個意象總是讓我抓狂

不去洛杉磯
意外投入台灣懷抱
在班機上，我被洛杉磯的魅力所煩
有一天，我還在台灣
走過饒河街夜市
我頂上是寺廟般的拱門
到處都是商店和食堂
包子、豬肉和蔬菜
我品嘗金牌台灣啤酒
台北的饒河市場多麼精彩！
真是萬事俱備的地方！
我全忘掉洛杉磯啦

神住在台灣

神愛台灣住在台灣
有玉山、秀姑巒溪、達芬尖山
祂邁步走下太魯閣峽谷
沐浴在立霧溪清水中
為了悅目，他觀賞
晨旭在十分瀑布
層層水面上創造出
千變萬化色彩。

神愛台灣住在台灣
清晨時分
祂在東埔村
喝地熱溫泉水。
祂在春天想要大飽眼福時
搜尋盛開的櫻花樹
和武陵農場生機勃勃的樹葉
然後想瀏覽台北市全景時
就攀登七星山
觀看祂的子民和活動。

神住在台灣愛台灣
自我創造十八羅漢山
在那裡祂可以找到獼猴
和赤腹松鼠
是祂自己精心創造的動物

祂有時會忘形於梨山風景區
觀賞祂創造的秀麗景色
瀑布、蘋果、桃和梨
以致迷失自己，
祂有時可以在阿里山森林
寧靜中過夜
神愛台灣住在台灣。

祂有時會忘形於梨山風景區
觀賞祂創造的秀麗景色
瀑布、蘋果、桃和梨
以致迷失自己，
祂有時可以在阿里山森林
寧靜中過夜
神愛台灣住在台灣。

台灣

我站在你面前
台灣呀
我翻開你像圖畫書
一頁又一頁
一章又一章
閱讀你
逐行
逐段
滿心歡喜
其中插圖
暢飲
你照片中的
水
我翻開一頁
即翻開另一次
走過大肚王國
清朝
走過東寧王國
國姓爺府
到福爾摩莎共和國
我繼續翻開你像圖畫書
台灣呀
一頁又一頁
一章又一章
逐行閱讀你
台灣呀
台灣呀

如果我繪妳

如果我繪妳
台灣呀
我會把妳繪成非洲女人
攜帶小葫蘆
在餵妳的孩子
我會繪妳
有強壯的背
堅挺的脖子
挺住殖民勢力
獲得勝利
成為世界最佳經濟體
我會把妳頭髮繪成
黑如灰燼
非洲的顏色
人民的熱情
陽光燦爛的臉龐
我會在妳的嘴唇上
加上笑容
善良和人性的象徵
我會在妳臉頰繪酒窩
美麗和魅力的
象徵
我會在妳的門牙上
創造間隙
非洲美麗的象徵
我會在妳的右臂上

安置鏢槍
另一隻手臂上擺盾牌
二者都由豹皮製成
那是權力、堅韌
和勝利的象徵
我會在妳的腰部
放美麗的非洲珠串
在妳走路時創造管弦樂
並裝飾妳的風景
我會在妳手腕上繪手鐲
在妳脖子上繪金鍊條
那是財富和
祝福豐饒的的象徵
如果我繪妳
台灣呀
我會把妳繪成非洲女人

台北雨

台北雨
就像看不見的鏢槍
射落下來
雲膜上不留刮痕
射來時
無需在宇宙打洞
或與天空結怨
雨親吻大地
很是歡喜
擁抱土壤
為蘭花帶來歡樂
對林地微笑
給動物生命
人們制定儀式
慶祝雨臨。

台灣蘭花

台灣呀
真是蘭花之鄉
蘭花到處綻放
沿路
林木間
四重溪脈葉蘭
和天麻花束
守在後院
玉山一葉蘭
點綴人行道和路邊
台灣呀
真是蘭花之鄉
劍心蘭
到處綻放
長腳羊耳蒜
和台灣香莢蘭花束
為街道塗上色彩
星星般的
春蘭
充滿花園
台灣呀
真是蘭花之鄉

楓葉

我願留居在台灣
直到十月或十一月
或十二月
等到秋天
在這壯麗季節
飲甜美空氣
洗刷見證過
楓葉的經驗
去看落葉
去感受幸福
興奮
自然魅力

我願留居在台灣
更多一點，更久一點
去南投奧萬大露營
睡在動植物群中
看紅色和黃色
體驗溫泉、烤肉
坐在汐止拱北殿外面
閉眼祈禱
在幻象中看到
觀世音菩薩、關公
和土地公的肉身
然後坐直
此時看到楓樹轉紅

走進烏來森林
風景如畫
站在橋上觀看
全世界都在我面前
變紅和淡黃色

我願住在台灣
更多幾天，更多幾個月
沿著樹林散步
走入太平山森林
品味連綿起伏的風景
點綴紫葉楓樹
攀登誘人的拉拉山
觀賞紅檜樹林
令人驚嘆的深紅色景觀
也帶我去一座小山頂
馬那邦山
令人屏息的風景
讓我和布農族人聊天
聆聽他們的歌聲和故事

我願留居在台灣更長久些
直到十月或十一月
或十二月
等到秋天
來洗刷我自己
一粒彩色球
淡黃和深紅色

夜幕降臨台北

世界分水嶺。
上帝和天使從七星山觀看
神聖力量吞噬感官
天際線深紅色
傾盆大雨是藍色
在沉默冥想
樹木和山丘彼此
談愛訴情
月亮向海低語
大海傾聽變得溫柔
夜空上的群星
潤濕愛情乳白淚水
向玉山訴說昔日祕密
台北夜裡寂靜無聲
人民安靜、悄悄打鼾
小孩不會哭鬧
貓頭鷹不會像肯亞那樣
在山坡嚎叫
因為吱吱喳喳聲
被溫柔的風消音啦
濁水溪也已入睡
一切靜息，就像被遺忘的夢。

台北一位老翁

我在台北
曾經遇見過
一位老翁
李魁賢
愛的皺紋
在臉上橫衝直撞
學識枴杖
緊握在
佈滿血管的手中
他的灰髮智慧
聚攏到
頭頂帽子裡
他的神聖天性
他的虔誠態度
可以在他的語調中
滿溢聽到
這位老翁
就是我在台北市
所遇見的
李魁賢

我想要離開台灣（一）

我怕，這數字四
我急忙想要離開台灣
我在公車上坐第四位置
我住在四樓
第四位排隊用餐
我怕
我只想要離開台灣
我的手機號碼十位數字中有4
我今年54歲
有四首詩要讀
我的房間號碼是4
我怕，天呀！我怕，我真怕
我只想要離開台灣
現在是四點鐘下午茶時間
有四位朋友和我
一起坐在四號餐桌
天呀！我簡直怕啦，天呀！
我只是怕，天呀！
我只想要離開台灣
我家有四位兄弟姊妹
我的車牌號碼是 KBZ 444N
我們房屋總共有四間臥室
天呀，我怕，天呀！我怕
我只想要離開台灣
昨晚我買四支筆
和四本筆記簿

我今天下午4點要上節目
啊，這號碼四，天呀！
我怕，天呀，我怕！我真怕
我只想要急忙離開台灣
我怕，天呀，我怕，天呀！
我只想要離開台灣
這號碼四一天呀，我怕！
我只想要離開台灣

我今天下午4點要上節目
啊，這號碼四，天呀！

我想要離開台灣（二）

我想要離開台灣
要回家
去找陽光
去找黃昏細雨
踩在泥路上
弄髒我的鞋子
在台灣沒有泥路
道路都已鋪上柏油

我想要離開台灣
要回家
夜裡去看螢火蟲
去聽蟋蟀唧唧唧唧叫
去聆聽群鳥
在巢內歌唱
還有風輕輕吹過
一如往常
我在台北沒有看到
任何螢火蟲

我想要離開台灣
要回家
投向我的妻子
聽她夜晚如何打鼾
聽她如何打嗝
聽她笑、聽她哭

在爐邊
聽她講故事
講她講夢想的祕密
此時此刻，我無法到她身邊
只能憑我的願望和想像

我想要離開台灣
要回家
去聽鄰居兒童
喧鬧
和尖叫聲
為紙團爭搶
玩捉迷藏
而且互相戲弄
這裡的鄰居靜悄悄

我想要離開台灣
要回家
去看鬥牛比賽
看動物如何晃角
互相激怒
喜愛村民瘋狂
歡呼
爭吵變成打架
人民狼狽奔跑
全村動盪
最後慶賀公牛英雄
在台灣這裡
我們沒有鬥牛
我們只有火車和汽車呼嘯而過

如果我必須住在台灣

如果我必須住在台灣
我寧願住在南投
這裡有溪水緩緩流過
貫穿樹林
向下
流入日月潭
那裡有群鳥在忘憂森林裡
柔聲唱歌
有蟋蟀
唧唧唧唧的聲音
從阿里山森林
幽幽散發出來

我寧願住在宜蘭
我可以看到火車經過
在林木間穿梭
公車蜿蜒穿越
進入太平山森林

我想要住在台北
那裡路面都已鋪好柏油
沒有泥巴會弄髒我的鞋子
那裡建築物高聳
觸及天際線

English Translation

I Don't Want to Go to Taiwan

I don't want to go to Taiwan
I am not apathetic enough
To go to Taiwan
It would be like
walking through a grave of tears
strewn with a gun of bones
and a bullet of myriad skulls

It would be like exhuming
the flesh and bones of heroes
Chiang Kai-shek, Mao Zedong
and injecting my body
with a nauseating pain of memories

I don't want to go to Taiwan
I am not cold-hearted enough
To go to Taiwan.
It would be like
waking up the spirits of
Koo Chen-fu and Lin Hsien-tang
and rendering them restless
I don't want to disturb dead souls
in their eternal resting abode
and make Taiwan shed tears again

It would be like
opening the grave of Ńg Kí-lâm
and peeking into the dark hole
rendering him unease and restless
I don't want to arouse the history of Taiwan
the struggle for independence and freedom

Truly, I don't want to go to Taiwan
I will easily get moved to tears
If I visit Taiwan
It would be like
re-igniting the taboo issue of independence
getting Su Beng back to the streets
for activism and protests
evading bullets from police
the arrests and tortures.

It would be like
bringing Su Beng from the graves
and attempt to assassinate Chiang Kai-shek
A very dangerous affair
I don't want to tolerate these memories
that display before me a shadow of Su Beng

Indeed, I hate going to Taiwan
I don't want to run its history
It would be like
bringing Peng Ming-min to live
forming his popular outfit
"A Declaration of Formosan Self-salvation"
To have him arrested, jailed
then later pardoned
sending him into exile
I can't stand the dark memories of Taiwan

It would be like
taking Taiwan back to
"The Democratic State of China-Taiwan"
And having Lei Chen
stand on the podium of history
to speak on the independence plan.
I don't want to go to Taiwan
I am not sufficiently callous
I am sensitive and can shed tears.

Landing in Taiwan

The plane seems to be biting back
At itself, shivering, belching along
A roar comes through, a wail and a buzz
Suppose it crushes — oh my!
Suppose the fuselage loosens
And falls apart? Or, one wing weakens
Or a flap flops, or a slat splits
Or, one spoiler comes apart?
Oh, my! — We shall all see ghosts
I hear a tremble, the fuselage shaking
It is like the whole thing is breaking
Listen to the loud sound from the rudder
The flaps and the aileron, the cockpit
Tearing the bowels of the clouds
Furs, cotton and sisals fly by
We float in the empty darkness
The engine wailing and fighting
Ouch! – The thing suddenly drops
An old woman seated next to me
Quickly presses her legs against the seat
In an attempt to hold the plane in place
Oh, my! — listen to the eerie roar
The trembling and the creaking
Who will ever know we were up here?
Taipei will never know our names
They will not listen to our poems

We shall be lost in the cosmos
Oh, my! — suppose the stabilizers drop off?
The pilot will not control the plane
Oh my! —I fear— oh my!
We shall sway, swerve and stray
Maybe drop into the ocean and drown
Or plunge into the forest be devoured by animals
Ouch! — Another sudden descending!
My heart misses a beat — Oh my!
My intestines coil inside my stomach
I hold tight onto the seat-belt
I pray— or do I want to cry?
I tremble as the fuselage shakes
The sound of the engine intensify
Suppose we plunge into the Bermuda triangle?
Oh, my! Oh my! Oh my! — I fear!
We shall vanish, disappear without a trace
There will be no wreckage, no survivors
Oh pilot, our good pilot, I beseech you
Check for that famous agonic line
I hear you should not compensate
For magnetic compass variation — is it so, Pilot?
Oh my! -- fear engulfs my whole being
We are likely to be swallowed by a rogue wave
Oh my! — a sudden tremble, a slow turn of the plane
A jerk, a shake and blood freezes inside my veins
The fuselage seems to be tearing apart
Ouch! — the thing drops suddenly again
I hold onto my seat, shut my eyes and pray
The old woman tightens her fingers on the seat

And shuts her eyes in utter terror
She is crying — or probably praying
The clouds are now clear — a great relief
The rays of the sun comes through
Another tremble, and finally a big bang
The tires scream along the runway
The fury of the plane could be heard
As its overstretched patience bursts out
Taiwan, here comes our Africa!
Taiwan, here comes our poetry!

The Language of Taiwan People

your language
drops out like cowrie shells
on a twig-made tray
Ching chong ching
a flurry of musical beats
a staccato of words
syllables hit the ear-drum with a thud
you can't miss the emphasis
the precision
the clarity
It is like a burst of bullets
coming out rapidly
continuously
and harder
upon the surface of the ear
danceable
drum-like
beautiful
sweet and romantic.

Tang Te-Chang

March 11th, 1947.
From a distant, KMT
Heard your heart-beat
Oh soul-brother
Sakai Tokushou
Although with a Japanese blood
You stood by us
Holding our flag high
Took in our spirit
And became one of us
Oh, brother Tokushou
Without uttering a word
Of betrayal, of disloyalty
You gave up your soul
Body, blood and spirit
For our independence
Tortured and humiliated
You gave up your breath
You died in Tainan
In the nation you loved most
Oh, brother Tokushoi
Fly high with the angels.

Immolation

(In memory of Cheng Nan-jung)

With your body and soul
your determined spirit
you baptized yourself with fire
turning into cinders
to prevent arrest
to protest against ROC

Like Chinese Kings
who could sacrifice animals
you immolated yourself
and offered your body
as a sacrificial lamb
so that we Taiwanese
could have freedom
democracy and power
You are still alive in us
Cheng Nan-jung

In Taiwan Dreams Grow on Trees

(For Fan Yu-Tzu, My Guide)

You are lucky to be born in Taiwan
where dreams grow on cobra saffron
and life and love
are painted on roses and daffodils
while resilience, like a phoenix
or, like in Jesus' death and resurrection
is retold on red poppies
You are lucky to be Taiwanese
and able to speak the musical language of the people
dance in the lantern festival
and honour the dead ancestors
relish yuanxiao and tangyuan
the wholeness and unity of families
reconciliation, peace and forgiveness
You are lucky to be living in Taiwan
where an old person is regarded as a purse
that holds jewels and gold
Where Kuei-shien Lee
a professor, is able to speak
and the youth like you
catch the creative Muse of the hills
and the wisdom of the rivers
You are lucky in Taiwan
where you observe Hell Banknote tradition

to support the dead ancestors
Where, in the Lunar New year,
you share in a sumptuous meal as families
where, during the funeral ceremonies,
the wandering spirits of the dead
are appeased, made harmless
by pole dancers and strippers.
You are lucky to be born in Taiwan
where the glamour and beauty of the sun
warm the hearts of the people
and the soft rain nourishes minds of children.

I didn't Plan to Come to Taiwan

I didn't plan to come to Taiwan
I had arranged a flight to NW Arizona
to see the large, deep river valley
where I could engage in hiking,
rafting and helicopter rides over the canyon
and take a bicycle ride on the South Rim.

But I changed my mind and came to Taiwan
Where I found the Sun Moon Lake
Shaped like a sun on the East
Shaped like a crescent moon on the west
when the sun rises, I noticed,
the sky turns pink and purple
Lalu, a small dot in the lake
-Oh, what an amazing natural beauty?
I have simply fallen in love with Taiwan.

Surely I didn't plan to visit Taiwan
Because I had this big excitement
of visiting California
to see Yosemite National Park
and enjoy the natural diversity
deep valleys, waterfalls, meadows
and giant sequoias – all these beauty!

But – ouch! -- I came to Taiwan instead
I visited Jiufen Old Street North of Taipei
I tasted a mystic aura – a hanging mist
I bought jewelry, pots, and ate
yu yuan, taro or yam balls
hong zhao ba wan, pork marinated in red wine
and *mua-chi,* glutinous rice cakes.
I am surely amazed being in Taiwan!

I didn't plan to visit Taiwan
I had planned to go to New York City
and see those famous skyscrapers
(Can Taiwan surely have such skyscrapers?)
watch cabaret shows, enjoy
top cuisines and nice city meals

But, oh my! I accidentally came to Taiwan
I regretted for having missed the NYC skyscrapers
But before long a surprise came along:
I sighted Taiwan's 101-story skyscraper
I was mesmerized, I almost lost my breath!
Lungshan Temple, too, came rolling
cascading waterfall, koi fish pond
I forgot all about the NYC skyscrapers

I could not wish to be in Taiwan
But to be in Utah by all means
visit the Zion National Park
and have a breathtaking view:
steep red cliffs, the Virgin River
try hiking a little, go horseback riding
canyoneering and bicycling -- all these!

Unfortunately the wind blew me to Taiwan
On arrival, I wondered what I came to do here!
With a small attitude, a small sneer on my face
I visited Taroko National Park
Wow! What a stunning landscape!
I explored an eternal Spring Shrine
and marvelled at the monstrous
coastal Qingshui Cliffs
walked on the iconic Cimu Bridge
I was left tongue-tied, breathless
I became bewildered being in Taiwan!

I first had a dream of going to Washington DC
to see the famous White House
savour its well-constructed roads
visit the Smithsonian National Air
Space Museum and the Tidal Basin
watch a play at The John F. Kennedy
Center for the Performing Arts.

But, as it is, God flew me to Taiwan
But really, what in Taiwan can beat Washington?
While pondering on this, I arrived in Kaohsiung City
Oh God, my heart missed a beat, jaws dropped!
I marvelled at the beautiful harbour views
Cheng Ching Lake, dotted with tiny islands,
the breath-taking Shoushan Mountain
I bumped into monkeys on the paths
Oh beautiful Kaohsiung City!
What can match you, oh Kaohsiung!
I forgot all about Washington DC

Los Angeles has always been my dream
The Hollywood thing we hear about
The Griffith Observatory
Battleship Iowa Museum
Los Angeles County Museum of Art
the antique cars at the Nethercutt Collection
This image always makes me mad

Instead of going to Los Angeles
I accidentally dropped into the arms of Taiwan
On my flight I was haunted by Los Angels' glamour
One day, while in Taiwan, I walked along
Raohe Street Night Market:
above me a temple-like arch
shops and canteens everywhere
buns, pork and vegetables
I tasted the golden Taiwan beer
What an amazing Raohe Market in Taipei!
what a place with everything!
I forgot all about Los Angeles.

God Lives in Taiwan

God loves and lives in Taiwan:
Jade, Xiuguluan and Dafenjian
He strolls down Taroko Gorge
bathes in the pure waters of the Liwu River
To entertain his eyes, he watches
a kaleidoscopic color, created in the
morning sunlight in the cascading waters
of the Shifen Waterfall.

God loves and lives in Taiwan
In the morning hours, he drinks water
in the village of Dongpu
from the geothermal hot springs.
and when he desires to feed his eyes in Spring,
he searches for the blooming cherry trees
and a vibrant foliage in Wuling Farm
He then climbs Mount Qixing
when he wants a sweeping view of Taipei
To watch upon his people and their activities.

God lives and loves Taiwan
His own creation, the Shihba Luohanshan,
is where he can find macaques
and red-bellied squirrels
animals he so lovingly created himself
He sometimes loses himself

in the ecstasy of Lishan Scenic Area
to watch the scenic view he created,
the waterfalls, apples, peaches, and pears
He sometimes can spend a night
in the tranquility of Alishan Forest
God loves and lives in Taiwan.

Taiwan

I stand before you,
oh Taiwan
and I open you like a picture book
page by page
chapter by chapter
reading you
through lines
and paragraphs
and relishing the illustrations
therein
drinking deeply
from the waters
of your photos
I open a leaf,
and I open another
walks through the Kingdom of Middag
Qing Dynasty
through the Kingdom of Tungning
House of Koxinga.
to the Republic of Formosa
I continue opening you like a picture book
oh Taiwan
page by page
chapter by chapter
reading you through lines
oh Taiwan
oh Taiwan.

If I Paint You

If I paint you
Oh Taiwan
I will paint you like an African woman
carrying *engondo,* a small calabash
which feeds your children
I will paint you
with a sturdy back
and a solid neck
that stood the colonial forces
and triumphed
to become the best economy in the world
I will paint your hair
black like ash
the colour of Africa
the warmth of your people
the sun-lit faces
I will place a smile
on your lips
a symbol of kindness and humanity
I will paint a dimple on your cheeks
a symbol of beauty
and charm
I will create a gap
in your front teeth
a symbol of Africa beauty
I will place a spear

on your right arm
a shield on your other arm
both made of a leopard skin
a symbol of power
resilience and triumph
I will place on your loins
beautiful African beads
to create an orchestra when you walk
and to decorate your landscape
I will paint a bangle on your wrists
and a gold chain on your neck
a symbol of wealth
and abundance of blessings
If I paint you
Oh Taiwan
I will paint you like an African woman.

The Rain in Taipei

The Rain in Taipei
Like invisible spears
come down
leaving no scratches on the cloud's membrane
It comes
without making holes on the cosmos
or having a vendetta with the sky
it kisses the earth
with such a delight
embracing its soil
bringing joy to the orchids
smile to the woodlands
life to the animals
people make rituals
to celebrate its arrival.

Orchids in Taiwan

What a land of orchids
Oh Taiwan
blooms and blooms of orchids
along the roads
among the woods
bouquets of Nervilia crociformis
and Gastrodia elata
in backyards
Hemipilia cruciate
dotting the pavements and curbs
What a land of orchids
Oh Taiwan
Blooms and blooms
of Tolumnia
bouquets of the Liparis condylobulbon
and the Vanilla somae
colouring the streets
the star-like
Cymbidium goeringii
filling gardens
what a land of orchids
Oh Taiwan!

Maple Leaves

I wish to stay in Taiwan
till October, or November
or December
to wait for autumn
and drink the sweet air
of this spectacular season
to wash through the experience
of witnessing the maple leaves
to see the falling foliage
and to feel the happiness
the excitement
the charm of nature

I wish to stay in Taiwan
a little more, a little longer
and camp at Nantou Aowanda
to sleep in the flora and fauna
to see the red and yellow
to experience hot springs, barbecues
to sit outside Xizhi Gongbei Temple
and close my eyes in prayer
and see in a vision
the body of Guanyin Bodhisattva,
Guan Gong, and the Earth God.
then sit upright
to now watch the maple trees turning red

Go into Wulai forest
a picturesque scene
stand on the bridge and see
the whole world in front of me
turn red and pale yellow

I wish to live in Taiwan
more days, more months
and walk along the woods
into Taiping Mountain forest,
savour in the rolling landscapes
dotted with purple-leafed maple trees.
climb up the alluring La-la mountain
to watch the red cypress forest,
a stunning crimson landscape
Take me to a miniature peaks, too
Manabang Shan
a breathtaking landscape
Let me talk to Bunun people
and listen to their songs and stories

I wish to stay longer in Taiwan
till October, or November
or December
to wait for autumn
to wash myself through
a pellet of colours
pale yellow and crimson red.

Nightfall in Taipei

A watershed of the world.
God and angels watch from the Shichisei
a divine power engulfs the senses
The skyline is crimson red
The rain that pours is blue in color
be silent and meditative
the trees and the hills talk
and tell each other of love
The moon whispers to the sea
and the sea listens and goes gentle
The stars above at night
wet with milky tears of love
whisper secrets of yore to the Yushan
Taipei is soundless at night
People snore quietly, stilly
and small children don't whimper
owls don't howl from hillsides
as they do in Kenya
sounds of chirps and twitters
are silenced by gentleness of wind
Zhuoshui River goes to sleep as well
It is all quiet like a forgotten dream.

An Old Man in Taipei

I once met
an old man
in Taipei
Kuei-shien Lee
wrinkles of love
zigzagged his face
a stick of knowledge
held tightly
in his vein-filled hand
his grey wisdom
was gathered
in the hat on his head
his divine nature
his godliness
could be heard
overflowing in the tone of his words
That is the old man
whom I met
in the city of Taipei
Kuei-shien Lee.

I Want to Leave Taiwan (I)

I fear, this number four
I urgently want to leave Taiwan
I am number four in the bus,
I stay on 4th floor
And four in the meal queue
I fear
I just want to leave Taiwan
My cellphone No. has 4s in the ten digits
And I am 54 years old
And has four poems to read
And my room number is 4
I fear, oh my! I fear, I really fear
I just want to leave Taiwan
It is four o'clock tea-time now
I have four friends seated with me
Restaurant table number four
Oh, my! I simply fear, oh my!
I Just fear, oh my!
I just want to leave Taiwan
I have four siblings back home
My car number plate is KBZ 444N
Our house has four bedrooms in total
Oh, my, I fear, oh my! I fear
I just want to leave Taiwan

I bought four pens last night
And four note-books
I will be performing at 4 pm today
Oh, this number four, oh my!
I fear, oh my, I fear! I really fear
I just want to leave Taiwan urgently
I fear, oh my, I fear, oh my!
I just want to leave Taiwan.
This number four- oh my, I fear!
I just want to leave Taiwan.

I Want to Leave Taiwan (II)

I want to leave Taiwan
and go home
to sunshine
to evening soft rain
walk on the mud
and smudge my shoes
there is no mud in Taiwan
roads are tarmacked

I want to leave Taiwan
and go home
to watch fireflies at night
and hear crickets chirp
and birds sing
from their nests
and the wind blowing gently
as it always does
I have not seen any fireflies
in Taipei

I want to leave Taiwan
and go home
to my wife
hear how she snores at night
how she belches
her laughter and cries

Listen to her stories
and secrets of her dreams
by the fireside
Currently, I can't reach her
but only in my wishes and imaginations

I want to leave Taiwan
and go home
to hear the din and screams
from children
in the neighbourhood
fighting over a paper-ball
playing hide-and-seek
and teasing each other
Here the neighbourhood is silent

I want to leave Taiwan
and go home
to see bull-fighting game
how the animals rock horns
and goad each other
enjoy the cheering
frenzy of village people
the brawl turning into a fight
and people running helter skelter
the village stir
and finally celebrating the hero-bull
Here in Taiwan
we have no bull-fighting
we only have the trains and cars zooming by.

If I Must Live in Taiwan

If I must live in Taiwan
Then I will prefer to live in Nantou
Where streams flow gently
through the woods
down
into the sun-moon Lake
Where birds sing
softly in Wangyu forest
and the chirps
of crickets
emanate tenderly
from the Alishan Forest

I will prefer to live in Yilan
where I can watch the train pass-by
among the woods
and buses snake their way through
into Taipingshan forest

I will desire to live in Taipei
where roads are tarmacked
and no mud can soil my shoes
where buildings rise up
and touch the skyline.

詩人簡介

克利斯多福．歐肯姆瓦（Christopher　　　Okemwa），肯亞基西（Kisii）大學文學教師，基斯特雷奇（Kistrech）　國際詩歌節創辦人兼總監。已出版詩集《鑼》（*The Gong*, 2010 年）、《煉獄之火》（*Purgatorius Ignis*, 2016 年，法文譯本）、《不祥的雲》（*Ominous Clouds*, 2018年，有挪威文、 芬蘭文、希臘文譯本）、《聖殤像》（*The Pieta*, 2019 年，亞美尼亞文譯本）、 《來自非裔加泰羅尼亞的愛》（*Love from Afro Catalonia*, 2020 年，加泰羅尼亞文譯本）、《詩選》（*Izabrane Pesme*, 2020 年，塞爾維亞文譯本）、《煉獄》（*Tisztítótűz*, 2020 年，匈牙利文譯本）、《牆壁與空曠空間之間》（*Between the Walls and Empty Space*, 2021 年 ，荷蘭出版）。歐肯姆瓦編過《疫情期間沉思：新冠病毒世界詩選》（*Musings During a Time of Pandemic: A World Anthology of Poems on COVID-19*, 2020年）、《我無法呼吸：社會正義詩選》（*I Can't Breathe: A Poetic Anthology of Social Justice*, 2021年）、《烏班圖歌舞藝人：非洲當代詩選》（*The Griots of Ubuntu: An Anthology of Contemporary Poetry from Africa*, 2022年） 、《走出孤立：堅韌、希望和勝利之世界詩選》（*Coming Out of Isolation: A World Anthology of Poems on Resilient, Hope and Triumph*, 2022年）、《來自樹林的聲音：東非及其他地區的詩選》（*Voices from the Woods: An Anthology of Poems from East Africa and Beyond*, 2023年）。歐肯姆瓦是基斯特雷奇國際詩歌節雜誌2013～2022年編輯，也是《在生命黑暗中：詩選集》（*In the Murk of Life: An Anthology of Poetry*, 2019年 ）的聯合編輯。

About the Poet

Christopher Okemwa is a literature teacher at the Kisii University in Kenya and the founder and director of the Kistrech International Poetry Festival. He has published poetry collections "*The Gong,* 2010", "*Purgatorius Ignis,* French version, 2016", "*Ominous Clouds,* in Norwegian, Finnish, and Greek versions, 2018", "*The Pieta,* Armenian version, 2019", "*Love from Afro Catalonia,* Catalan version, 2020", "*Izabrane Pesme,* Serbian version, 2020", "*Tisztítótüz,* Hungarian version, 2020", "*Between the Walls and Empty Space,* published in the Netherlands, 2021". Okenmwa has compiled various an anthologies including "*Musings During a Time of Pandemic: A World Anthology of Poems on COVID-19, 2020*", "*I Can't Breathe: A Poetic Anthology of Social Justice, 2021*", "*The Griots of Ubuntu: An Anthology of Contemporary Poetry from Africa, 2022*", "*Coming Out of Isolation: A World Anthology of Poems on Resilient, Hope and Triumph, 2022*", "*Voices from the Woods: An Anthology of Poems from East Africa and Beyond, 2023*". Okemwa is the editor of the Kistrech International Poetry Festival magazine from 2013 to 2022, and is the co-editor of "*In the Murk of Life: An Anthology of Poetry, 2019*".

譯者簡介

李魁賢，1937年生，1953年開始發表詩作，曾任國家文化藝術基金會董事長，現任世界詩人運動組織副會長。已出版各種語文詩集62本，詩作在日本、韓國、加拿大、紐西蘭、荷蘭、南斯拉夫、羅馬尼亞、印度、希臘、立陶宛、美國、西班牙、巴西、蒙古、俄羅斯、古巴、智利、波蘭、尼加拉瓜、孟加拉、馬其頓、塞爾維亞、科索沃、土耳其、葡萄牙、馬來西亞、義大利、墨西哥、摩洛哥、哥倫比亞等國發表。英譯詩集有《愛是我的信仰》、《溫柔的美感》、《島與島之間》、《黃昏時刻》、《給智利的情詩20首》、《存在或不存在》、《感應》、《彫塑詩集》、《兩弦》、《日出日落》、《李魁賢英詩選集》、《如河暢流》、《如鼓擂鳴》、《太陽之子》。除台灣外，榮獲印度、蒙古、韓國、孟加拉、馬其頓、祕魯、蒙特內哥羅（黑山）共和國、塞爾維亞、美國等詩獎。

About the Translator

Lee Kuei-shien was born in Taipei, Taiwan in 1937, started to write poems in 1953, a retired Chairman of National Culture & Arts Foundation in Taiwan, now the vice president of Movimiento Poetas del Mundo founded in Chile in 2005. He has published 62 poetry books in different languages, some of them have been contributed in Japan, Korea, Canada, New Zealand, The Netherlands, Yugoslavia, Romania, India, Greece, Lithuania, USA, Spain, Brazil, Mongolia, Russia, Cuba, Chile, Poland, Nicaragua, Bangladesh, Macedonia, Serbia, Kosovo, Turkey, Portugal, Malaysia, Italy, Mexico, Morocco and Colombia. His poetry collections in English translation include *"Love is my Faith"*, *"Beauty of Tenderness"*, *"Between Islands"*, *"The Hour of Twilight"*, *"20 Love Poems to Chile"*, *"Existence or Non-existence"*, *"Response"*, *"Sculpture & Poetry"*, *"Two Strings"*, *"Sunrise and Sunset"*, *"Selected Poems by Lee Kuei-shien"*, *"As The River Flows"* and *"As The Drums Beats"* which are Volume I and II of *"Collected Poems by Lee Kuei-shien"*, and *"Son of the Sun"*. In addition to Taiwan, his achievement in poetry creation has been awarded internationally in India, Mongolia, Korea, Bangladesh, Macedonia, Peru, Montenegro, Serbia and USA so far.